This Notebook belongs to

____

____

Rabbi Zidni 'Ilma

"Oh My Lord!
Advance me in
knowledge"

(Ta-ha, 114)

Printed in Great Britain
by Amazon

b41a87c4-3d6d-464e-8ddd-3bb4ed6e8a68R01